THE BIG BOOK OF DINOSAURS

THE BIG BOOK OF DINOSAURS

ILLUSTRATED by BOB WALTERS

AN IMPRINT OF RUNNING PRESS
PHILADELPHIA • LONDON

Printed in China

9 8 7 6 5 4
Digit on the right indicates the number of this printing

Library of Congress Cataloging-in-Publication Number 00-135512

ISBN 0-7624-0720-4

Cover design by Bill Jones
Interior design by Bill Jones and Gwen Galeone
Illustrated by Bob Walters
Written by Don Glut and Gil King
Edited by Danielle McCole

This book may be ordered by mail from the publisher.
Please include $2.50 for postage and handling.
But try your bookstore first!

Running Press Book Publishers
125 South Twenty-second Street
Philadelphia, Pennsylvania 19103-4399

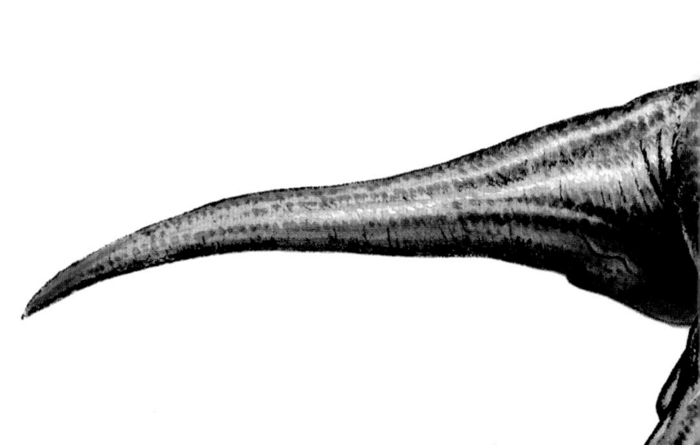

Table of Contents

What were the dinosaurs?

Contrary to popular perception, dinosaurs were among the most successful animals that ever lived. For more than 150 million years, they lived all over the earth, adapting to many different environments. They were spectacular in appearance—many of them every bit as strange as the monsters in mythology or the imagined inhabitants of alien worlds.

Museums are a great place to learn about Dinosaurs.

Their scientific name is Dinosauria, which means "terrible lizards." But the dinosaurs were not lizards, and not all prehistoric reptiles were dinosaurs. All dinosaurs were alike in certain ways. Dinosaurs did not creep or crawl like lizards or crocodiles. The pelvis, leg, ankle, and foot bones of all dinosaurs allowed them to stand upright like mammals. And all dinosaurs lived on land. (Flying reptiles or pterosaurs, and marine reptiles like plesiosaurs and mosasars were not dinosaurs, although they lived at the same time.)

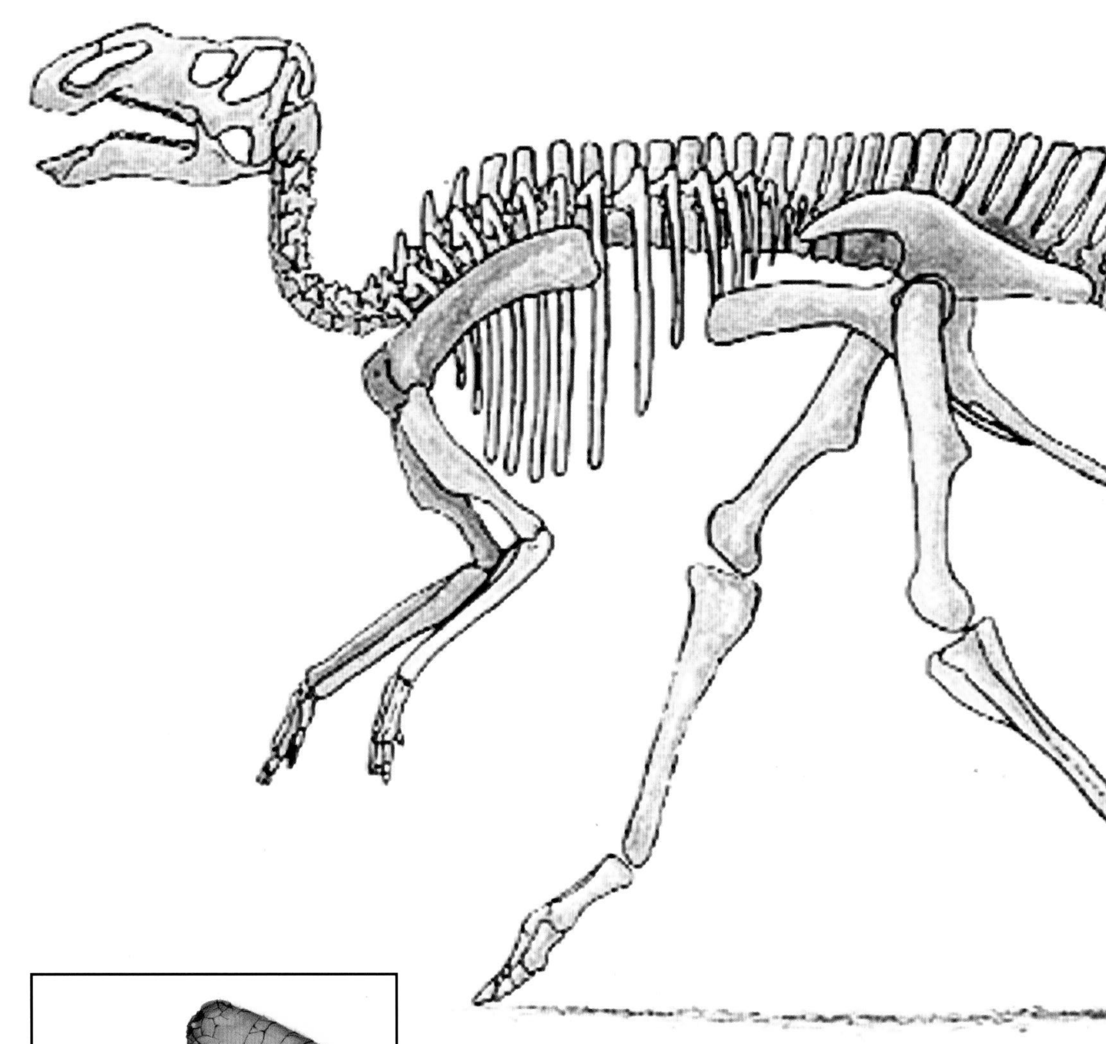

Skeleton of a Grypysaurus

Dinosaur Footprint and Eggs

Dinosaurs belong to a large group of "ruling reptiles" called Archosauria, and may have descended from an animal like Euparkaria, a reptile that lived long before the earliest dinosaurs. This 5 foot-long animal had a relatively large head (about 9 inches long) and walked on its hind legs. The Euparkaria resembled some or the earliest meat-eating dinosaurs and was a preview of what was to come!

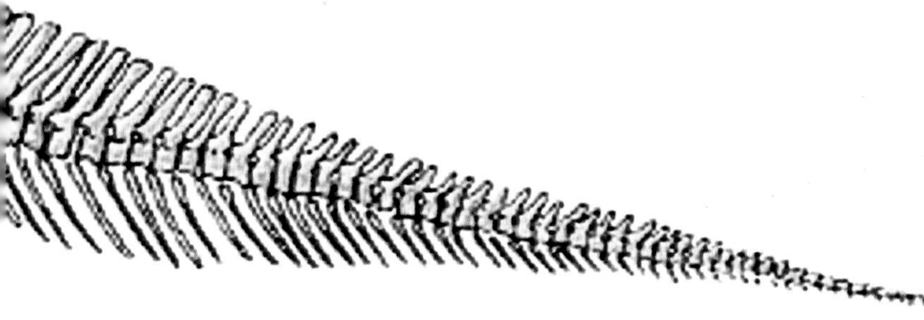

How do we know about them?

Without fossils, we would not know that dinosaurs ever existed. Fossil literally means "dug up." Dinosaur fossils include physical remains such as preserved bones and skin prints, and even traces (such as footprints, eggs, and dung). But the most collected dinosaur specimens are bones, which turned to stone, or petrified through the long process of fossilization.

The science of ancient living beings, called paleontology, is the study of fossils. Paleontologists who study vertebrae are dinosaur hunters and have a keen interest in the history of life on earth. They generally have years of training in their subject as well as other areas of science, such as geology and biology. Once fossils have been collected, paleontologists may write formal descriptions of them. If it is determined that these fossils constitute a new animal, the paleontologist gives it a new name.

Although paleontologists are best at interpreting fossil evidence, it's important to remember that some of our most spectacular dinosaur discoveries have been made by non-paleontologist, amateurs.

When and where did they live?

The dinosaurs lived during the "middle life"—the Mesozoic Era, which lasted from about 248 million years to 64 million years ago. Because Earth's lands, seas, and skies were dominated by reptiles during the Mesozoic, it is known as the "Age of Reptiles."

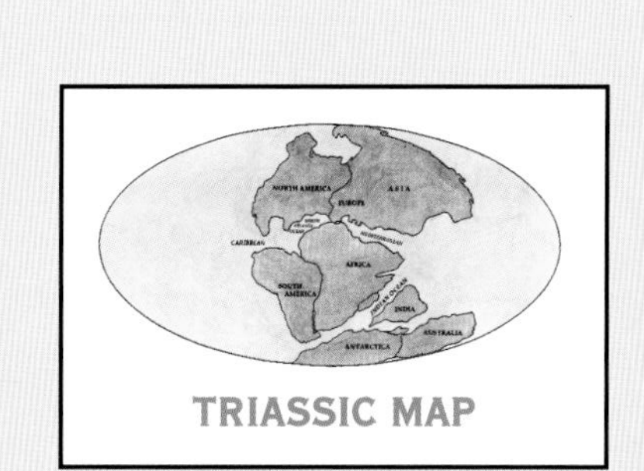
TRIASSIC MAP

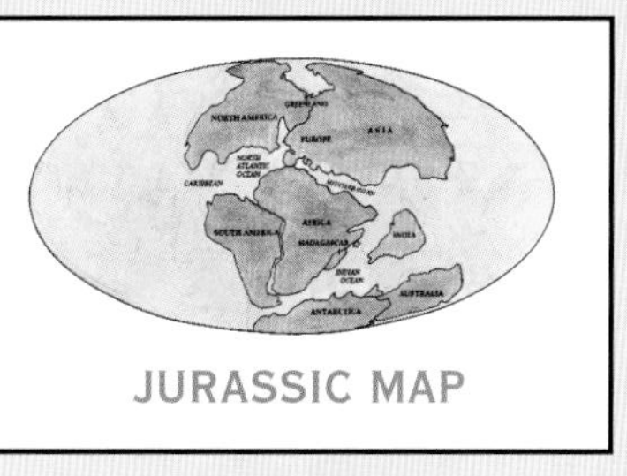
JURASSIC MAP

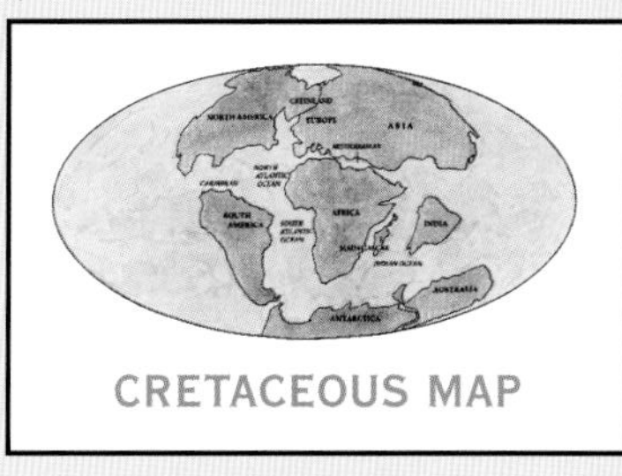
CRETACEOUS MAP

The geography of the Mesozoic Era was very different than it is today. During this era, the world's present continents were all part of one giant supercontinent called Pangaea. Over time, Pangaea was split apart by cracks that opened in the earth's crust, and the process of continental drift began. North America, Europe, and Asia were pulled away from South America, Africa, and Australia, and oceans flooded the gaps.

Geologists divide the Mesozoic Era into three periods—the Triassic (245 to 208 million years ago), the Jurassic (208 to 145 million years ago) and the Cretaceous (145 to 64 million years ago). Dinosaurs from the Triassic Era were free to wander in all directions, since there was no ocean to stop them from crossing the continent. By the time of the Cretaceous Era, the continents had split apart and each new continent was stocked with its own distinct variety of dinosaurs.

What are the different types of dinosaurs?

LIZARD-HIPPED DINOSAURS

All Dinosaurs descended from reptiles called thecondonts, which first appeared on Earth during the Triassic period. But there are two major dinosaur groups—Saurischia and Ornithischia. In 1887, British geologist Harry Seeley found a way of dividing dinosaurs into these two basic groups or orders. The Saurischia are called "lizard-hipped" dinosaurs, even though dinosaurs are not closely related to lizards. Saurischian dinosaurs were named for the arrangement of their pelvic bones—in the Saurischian pelvis, as in a lizard's, the three pelvic bones radiate away from one another in different directions. This is just one major difference between Saurischians and Ornithischians or "bird-hipped" dinosaurs.

LIZARD HIP DETAIL

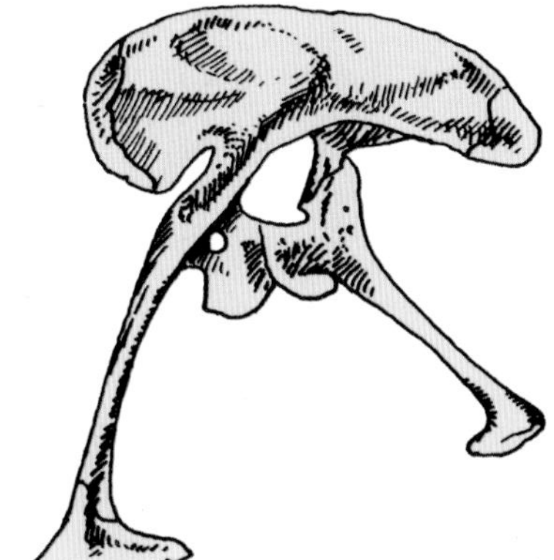

Dinosaurs whose hip bones were shaped like those of lizards fell into two different types—the agile, carnivorous theropods, and the slower-moving, plant-eating sauropods. Saurischians first appeared during the Late Triassic period and thrived until the Late Cretaceous. They ranged in size from the smallest of all dinosaurs (chicken-sized, like Compsognathus) to the most gigantic (more than 100 feet long, like Seismosaurus).

The reconstructed skeleton of a Tyrranosaurus Rex peers out over museum goers.

The first group of lizard-hipped dinosaurs to appear was the Therapoda, or "beast feet." These dinosaurs probably walked on their hind legs, since skeletons show that their front legs were too short to be effective for transportation. They had powerful legs, a long, muscular tail, and massive jaws with sharp teeth. Almost all theropods were meat-eaters, such as Allosaurus, Oviraptor and Tyrannosaurus.

The Sauropods, or "lizard feet" were the true giants of the Dinosauria. They walked on four strong, pillar-like legs, and some may have been able to rear up on their hind legs. Their tails ranged from very short, as in Brachiosaurus (whose tail was shorter than its neck) to very long, with the tail sometimes longer than the neck and rest of the body combined. Sauropod heads were quite small, usually less than two feet and housed the smallest brains of all dinosaurs, compared to body size. A sauropod brain could easily be held in one of your hands. Sauropods were also herbivores—plant-eating dinosaurs, such as Apatosaurus, Diplodocus and Seismosaurus.

BIRD-HIPPED DINOSAURS

Despite their name, the Ornithischia, or "bird-hipped" dinosaurs, were a large and diverse group that were even less birdlike than Saurischians. The Ornithischia were named for the bones of their pelvises, which were arranged like those of modern birds. Their pubis bone points downward and toward the tail, and the pelvis is wider than that of Saurischians. This may have enabled ornithischians to be more stable while moving. This group apparently branched off from the Saurischia sometime during the Late Triassic.

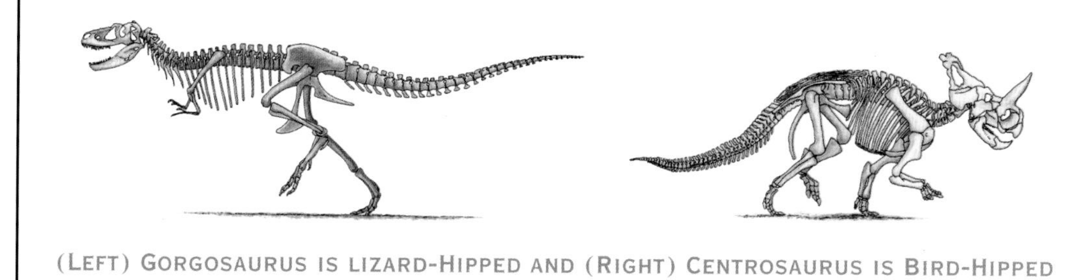

(Left) Gorgosaurus is lizard-hipped and (Right) Centrosaurus is Bird-Hipped

Ornithischia are divided into five types–ankylosaurs, ceratopsians, ornithopods, pachycephalosaurs and stegosaurs. All ornithischians had a horn-covered beak-like bone called a "predentary" at the front of the mouth, a useful tool for cropping vegetation. Ornithischians were herbivorous, and they ranged in size from the 4-foot long armored dinosaur, Scutellosaurus, to the 40-foot long duck-billed dinosaur Saurolophus. Some walked on their hind legs, some on all fours, and some on both. Most had flat cheek teeth at the sides and back of their mouths for chewing vegetation, and their pouch-like cheeks held food in their mouths as they chewed.

Bird Hip Detail

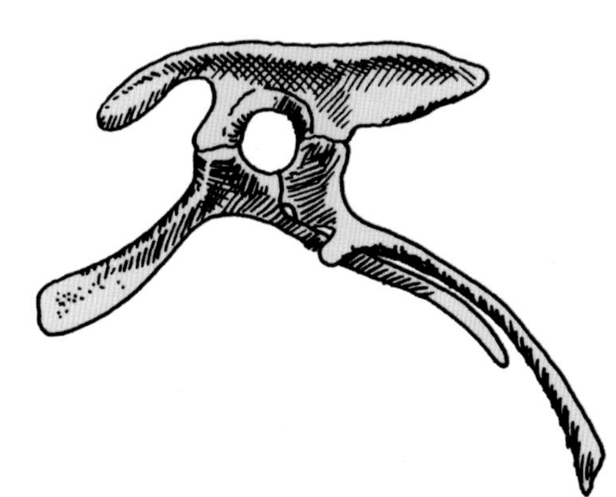

Ornithischians also had bigger stomachs than saurischians. These features allowed them to better chew plants and to keep them in their stomachs longer for improved digestion.

There was a lot of variety among ornithischians, more so than among the lizard-hipped dinosaurs. Some ornithischians sported flashy head crests, horns, or other ornamentation, while some of them had body armor, like plates and scutes. The ornithischians were among the last of the dinosaurs to die out.

DINOSAUR TIME LINE

TRIASSIC PERIOD

245–208 Million Years BC

JURASSIC PERIOD

208–145 Million Years BC

CRETACEOUS PERIOD

145–64 Million Years BC

Therapods

HERRARASAURUS
her-ar-a-sar-us

Lizard HIPPED

Meaning: *Victorino Herrara's lizard*
Group: *Therapoda*
Size: *3.5 to 17 feet long*
Time Period: *Late Triassic*
Where found: *Argentina*

Herrerasaurids were agile, quick-moving creatures. We know this because their thigh bones were shorter than their lower-leg bones, indicative of running animals. Their foreclaws were well designed for catching prey. Holding their victim in their hinged jaws, these early dinosaurs tore into its flesh with long, serrated teeth.

EORAPTOR
e-o-rap-tor

Lizard HIPPED

Meaning: *Dawn Thief*
Group: *Therapoda*
Size: *3 feet long*
Time period: *Late Triassic*
Where found: *Argentina*

Eoraptor was a small meat-eater, but a clever hunter forced by its size to prey mainly upon small animals. In bold moments, it may have snatched up the young of larger animals—but Eoraptor had to be careful. The main meat-eaters of its day were narrow-nosed reptiles called phytosaurs, some of which grew to more than 19 feet long–six times longer than Eoraptor. Dinosaurs were secondary citizens of their world at this time. It was not yet their turn to rule the Earth.

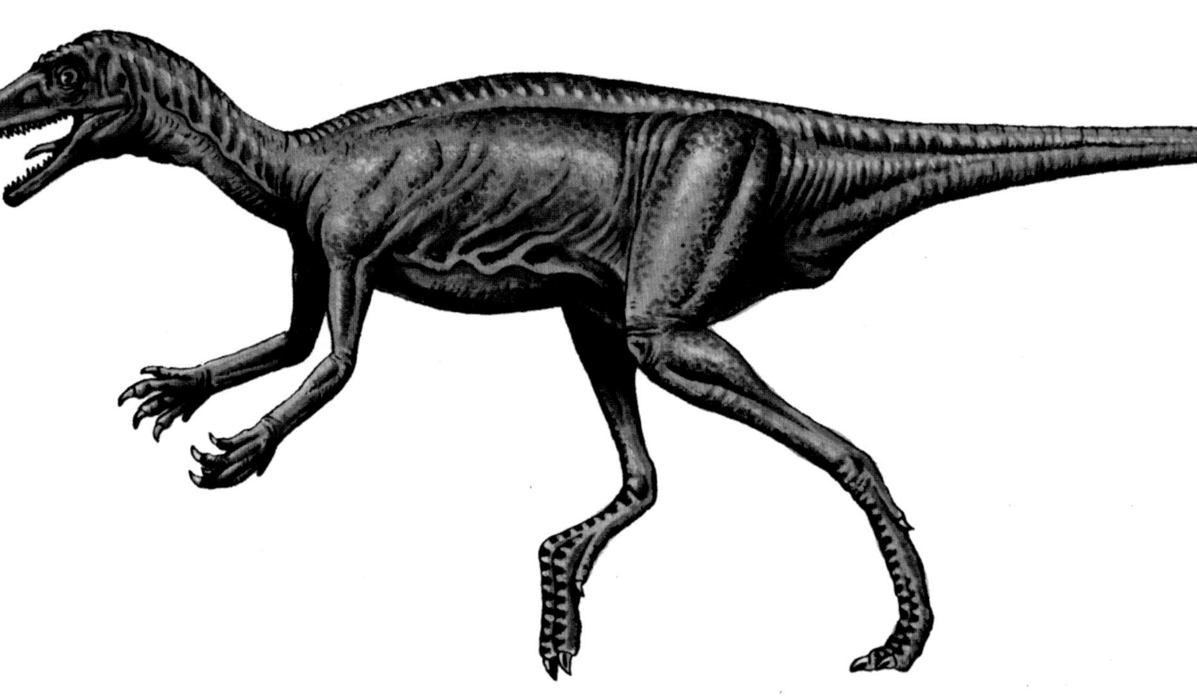

Prosauropods

AMMOSAURUS
am-uh-sar-us

Lizard HIPPED

Meaning: *Sandy Ground Lizard*
Group: *Prosauropoda*
Size: *14 feet long*
Time period: *Early Jurassic*
Where found: *Connecticut, Nova Scotia, Arizona*

Ammosaurus was a large plant-eater, with a small head and long neck. Discovered by quarry men over a century ago, only the back half of this dinosaur was salvaged—the rest was contained in sandstone block which was demolished and built into a bridge in Connecticut. However, in 1969, another sandstone bridge nearby was dismantled, leading to the discovery of more skeletal remains of Ammosaurus.

PLATEOSAURUS
pla-tee-o-sar-us

Lizard HIPPED

Meaning: *Flat Lizard*
Group: *Prosauropoda*
Size: *27 feet long*
Time period: *Late Triassic*
Where found: *Germany, Switzerland, France*

Plateosaurus walked on all fours, but could probably rear up on its hind legs when it had to reach high-growing vegetation or to defend itself. Plateosaurus had a large hand claw that could rake foliage and could even be used as a weapon.

Sauropods

MAMENCHISAURUS
mah-men-chi-sar-us

Lizard HIPPED

Meaning: *Brook Lizard*
Group: *Sauropoda*
Size: *70 feet*
Time Period: *Late Jurassic*
Where found: *China*

Mamenchisaurus was Asia's largest known dinosaur, with an extremely long neck (35 feet), the longest of any terrestrial animal known to man. With nineteen cervical vertebrae, Mamencisaurus's neck made up half his length.

Sauropods

CAMARASAURUS
kam-uh-ruh-sar-us

Lizard HIPPED

Meaning: *Chamber Lizard*
Group: *Sauropoda*
Size: *Over 60 feet*
Time Period: *Late Jurassic*
Where found: *Colorado, Utah, Wyoming, Portugal*

Camarasaurus is among the most common fossil finds in North America, especially the immature ones. This large, four-legged sauropod was solidly built with sturdy, thick front legs and large nostrils above his snout.

DIPLODOCUS
di-plo-duh-kus

Lizard HIPPED

Meaning: *Double-folded bearing-beam*
Group: *Sauropoda*
Size: *88 feet long*
Time period: *Late Jurassic*
Where found: *Colorado, Wyoming, Utah, Montana*

Diplodocus was one of the largest dinosaurs, with an elongated snout, nostrils on top of his head, and teeth only at the front of his mouth. Its tail tapered into a whip which could have been used as a weapon.

DIPLODOCUS SKULL

Sauropods

APATOSAURUS
a-pat-o-sar-us

Lizard HIPPED

Meaning: *Deceptive Lizard*
Group: *Sauropoda*
Size: *75 feet long*
Time period: *Late Jurassic*
Where found: *Colorado, Utah, Wyoming*

Once known as Brontosaurus, ***Apatosaurus*** is probably the most famous dinosaur of all. This massive dinosaur is a member of the sauropod subgroup Diplodocidae. Diplodocids were gigantic and weighed 30 tons or more. Some were extremely long, reaching lengths of more than 100 feet. Their tails were long and tapered, sometimes ending in a "whiplash." When snapped or cracked these tails served as weapons to fend off hungry therapods.

BRACHIOSAURUS
bra-key-o-sar-us

Lizard HIPPED

Meaning: *Arm Lizard*
Group: *Sauropoda*
Size: *80 feet long*
Time Period: *Late Jurassic-Early Cretaceous*
Where found: *Colorado, Utah, Wyoming; Tanzania, Algeria, Africa; Portugal*

Brachiosaurus had a very long neck, about as long as the rest of its body and tail combined. Its front legs were longer than its hind legs, so its back sloped down towards its tail. This raised the front part of the animal so that it could reach vegetation growing on trees as tall as four-story buildings. Until recently, giants such as these were thought to be the biggest of all dinosaurs. Now, however, we know of even larger animals.

Sauropods

A stampede of *Camarasaurus* persued by a pack of *Allosaurs.*

Ornithopods

OTHNEILIA
oth-nee-lee-uh

Meaning: *Othniel (Charles Marsh)*
Group: *Ornithopoda*
Size: *4.6 feet long*
Time period: *Late Jurassic*
Where found: *Colorado, Utah, Wyoming*

Othneilia had small skulls and walked on their rear legs. A plant-eating dinosaur, Othneilia also had a hind foot with slim digits and a functional first digit. Though lightly built, their hind legs were quite powerful.

HETERRODONTOSAURUS
het-er-o-don-to-sar-us

Meaning: *Mixed-tooth Lizard*
Group: *Ornithopoda*
Size: *3 feet long*
Time period: *Late Triassic*
Where found: *South Africa*

Heterodontosaurus had two, long, tusk-like teeth, in addition to many smaller teeth. Such teeth appear in meat-eating animals, but Heterodontosaurus's teeth may have acted as defensive weapons, like the oversized teeth of wild pigs today. They may also have been used for digging, or for cutting food. Some scientists believe that only Heterodontosaurus males had these tusks and used them to establish their dominance over other males and to attract females.

Therapods

CERATOSAURUS
sir-rat-uh-sar-us

Meaning: *Horned Lizard*
Group: *Therapoda*
Size: *20 to 30 feet long*
Time period: *Late Jurassic*
Where found: *Colorado, Utah, Oklahoma, East Africa*

Ceratosaurus, a large ceratosaur, had a prominent nose horn. Because it needed no weapons other than its teeth, claws, and size, this horn was probably not used as a weapon. Male Ceratosaurus may have used their horns in butting contests to establish dominance, territory, and mates.

COMPSOGNATHUS
Komp-sog-nay-thus

Meaning: *Elegant Jaw*
Group: *Therapoda*
Size: *Approximately 28 inches long*
Time Period: *Late Jurassic*
Where found: *Germany, France*

One of the most complete and best-preserved dinosaur skeletons is a specimen of ***Compsognathus,*** discovered in limestone in Germany. The development of this specimen's bones show that it was a juvenile when it died—a mature adult would have been bigger. Preserved within the stomach area of this specimen was the skeleton of a small lizard, so we know what this Compsognathus individual enjoyed for its last meal.

Therapods

SINRAPTOR
sin-rap-tor

Meaning: *Chinese Raider*
Group:*Therapoda*
Size: *21 feet*
Time period: *Late Jurassic*
Where found: *China*

Sinraptor was the dominant carnivore of its time. Large, ferocious and bearing sharp teeth and claws, Sinraptor was a particulary fearsome "fighting dinosaur" whose preserved skull shows evidence of wounds perhaps inflicted by another Sinraptor.

YANGCHUANOSAURUS
yang-choo-an-uh-sar-us

Meaning: *Yangchuan (A district of Szechuan Province, China) Lizard*
Group: *Therapoda*
Size: *33 feet long*
Time period: *Late Jurassic*
Where found: *China*

Yangchuanosaurus was a large meat-eating dinosaur, similar to Allosaurus in that it had large jaws and sharp, pointed teeth. With a double horn-like ridge on its head, Yangchuanosaurus may have had a crest which may have been colored and used for display.

Therapods

COELOPHYSIS
see-luh-fy-sis

Lizard HIPPED

Meaning: *Hollow Form*
Group: *Therapoda*
Size: *9 feet long*
Time period: *Late Triassic*
Where found: *New Mexico, Utah, Arizona*

Coelophysis had a small head, very strong jaws, sharp teeth, long neck and rather long front limbs. Discovered by Edwin H. Colbert in a "dinosaur graveyard" located at the Ghost Ranch site in New Mexico, this meat-eating dinosaur is believed to have lived or associated in large groups.

MEGALOSAURUS
meg-uh-luh-sar-us

Lizard HIPPED

Meaning: *Big Lizard*
Group: *Therapoda*
Size: *25 feet long*
Time period: *Middle Jurassic*
Where found: *England, France, Portugal*

Megalosaurus was a large, meat eating dinosaur which resembled Allosaurus. With its giant head, long jaws, double-edged teeth and short forelimbs, Megalosaurus also had a thick neck and robust upper arms.

Therapods

SAUROPHAGANAX
sor-o-fa-gan-ex

Meaning: *Lizard-Eater Master*
Group: *Therapoda*
Size: *49 feet long*
Time period: *Late Jurassic*
Where found: *Oklahoma*

Saurophaganax was unearthed in the 1930s in Oklahoma and very few skeletal remains were discovered. However, scientists believe this gigantic dinosaur was very similar to Allosaurus, only a much larger predator.

SYNTARSUS
sin-tar-sus

Meaning: *With Flat Foot*
Group: *Therapoda*
Size: *10 feet long*
Time period: *Early Jurassic*
Where found: *Zimbabwe, Arizona*

Syntarsus was a rather small, two-legged meat-eater with a small head, fairly long neck and a lightly built body. It had large hands with three well developed, functional and opposable fingers with sharp claws.

Therapods

Two *Dilophosauruses* crossing a mudflat.

DILOPHOSAURUS
dye-lo-fuh-sar-us

Meaning: *Two-crested Lizard*
Group: *Therapoda*
Size: *20 feet long*
Time period: *Early Jurassic*
Where found: *Arizona*

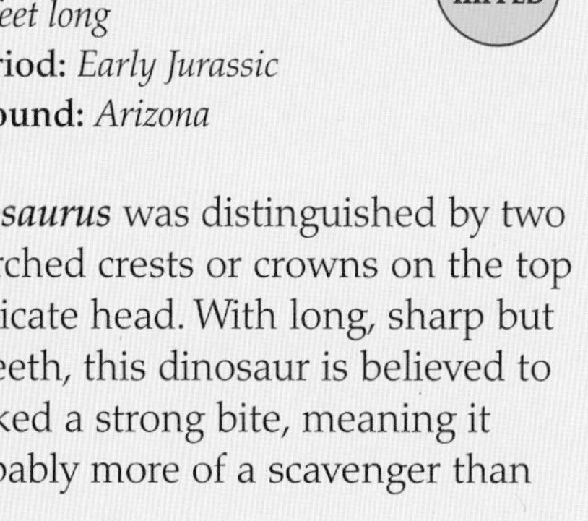

Dilophosaurus was distinguished by two highly arched crests or crowns on the top of its delicate head. With long, sharp but skinny teeth, this dinosaur is believed to have lacked a strong bite, meaning it was probably more of a scavenger than a hunter.

Therapods

ALLOSAURUS
al-o-sar-us

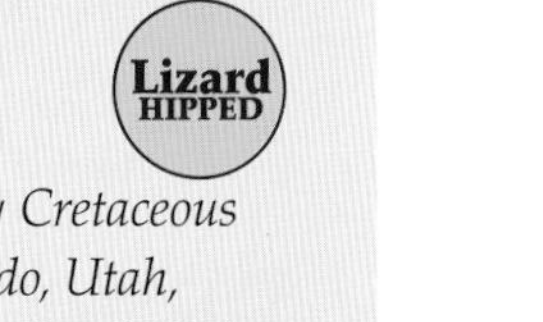

Meaning: *Different Lizard*
Group: *Therapoda*
Size: *30 feet long*
Time period: *Late Jurassic–Early Cretaceous*
Where found: *Wyoming, Colorado, Utah, Montana, Oklahoma, New Mexico, South Dakota, Australia, Tanzania*

Allosaurus had a head that was three feet long with 4 to 6-inch teeth. It was a very dangerous predator with powerful three-fingered hands, each with a 6-inch claw. This huge dinosaur can be identified by the small "horns" above its eyes.

ALLOSAURUS SKULL

ORNITHOLESTES
or-nith-o-less-tees

Lizard
HIPPED

Meaning: *Bird Robber*
Group: *Therapoda*
Size: *6 feet long*
Time period: *Late Jurassic*
Where found: *Wyoming, Utah*

Ornitholestes was a graceful, lightly built animal. It had a long tail that helped to stabilize it when it ran after prey or from larger theropods. Its skull shows traces of what may have been a small horn over its nose. This may have been used to attract mates or to win territory.

Therapods

Ornitholestes being pursued by the much larger *Allosaurus*.

Armor

SCUTELLOSAURUS
Skoo-tuh-luh-sar-us

Meaning: *Little Shield Lizard*
Group: *Thyreophora*
Size: *4 feet long*
Time period: *Early Jurassic*
Where found: *Arizona*

Scutellosaurus was a primitive dinosaur with armor that was more devoloped than most dinosaurs of the early Jurassic period. With a very long tail, Scutellosaurus was mostly bipedal, with thin hind limbs, small feet and over 300 armor plates found with the namesake skeleton.

HUAYANGOSAURUS
hwye-ang-guh-sar-us

Meaning: *Hua Yang Guo Zhi (book from Jin Dynasty) Lizard*
Group: *Stegosauria*
Size: *13 feet long*
Time period: *Middle Jurassic*
Where found: *China*

The earliest known stegosaur was ***Huayangosaurus***. This dinosaur had two rows of small plates along its neck and back shaped like lances, and four tail spines. It also had teeth in the front of its mouth, a primitive feature not present in advanced stegosaurs.

Armor

STEGOSAURUS
steg-uh-sar-us

Meaning: *Roofed Lizard*
Group: *Stegosauria*
Size: *25 feet long*
Time period: *Late Jurassic*
Where found: *Colorado, Wyoming, Utah*

Lizard HIPPED

The best-known and largest stegosaur is, of course, ***Stegosaurus*** itself. This dinosaur wore two rows of bone plates, some 2 feet high and 2 feet wide, and four tail spikes that faced backwards. A stegosaur's tail spikes were formidable weapons. A stegosaur could swing its tail with enough force to fatally wound any therapod foolish enough to pursue it for dinner.

Stegosaurus defends himself with plates along his neck and back.

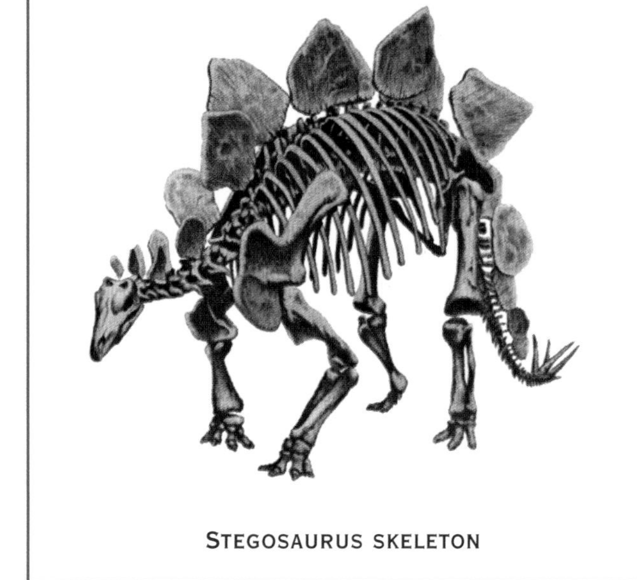

STEGOSAURUS SKELETON

Sauropods

REBBACHISAURUS
ruh-bach-I-sau-rus

Meaning: *Territory Lizard*
Group: *Sauropoda*
Size: *68 feet long*
Time period: *Early Cretaceous*
Where found: *Morocco, Niger*

Rebbachisaurus was a giant plant-eating dinosaur with a long tapering head and whiplike tail. He had large, spoon-shaped teeth and very strong hind legs with large claws. This giant also had a high-arched back, and perhaps even a sail with large, pointy spines.

Rebbachiasaurus is preyed upon by a *Gigantosaurus.*

SAUROPOSEIDON
sor-o-po-syd-on

Lizard HIPPED

Meaning: *Lizard Earthquake God*
Group: *Sauropoda*
Size: *60 feet tall*
Time period: *Mid Cretaceous*
Where found: *Oklahoma*

Sauroposeidon has the longest neck in fossil record, longer than even the Mamenchisaurus. The Sauroposeidon's individual vertebrae are up to 4 feet long, resembling a tree trunk more so than part of a dinosaur's neck.

Sauropods

AMARGASAURUS

a-mar-ga-sar-us

Lizard HIPPED

Meaning: *La Amarga (Argentina Canyon) Lizard*
Group: *Sauropoda*
Size: *33 feet long*
Time Period: *Early Cretaceous*
Where found: *Argentina*

Certainly one of the strangest looking of the dinosaurs, ***Amargasaurus*** was unique in that he had two rows of spines on his neck, back and tail vertebrae. Some scientists speculate that his unusual and elongated spine may have been a defensive trait, discouraging larger predetors from attacking his neck.

Therapods

CARCHARODONTOSAURUS
kahr-char-uh-don-tuh-sar-rus

Meaning: *Shark-toothed Lizard*
Group: *Therapoda*
Size: *27 feet long*
Time period: *Early to Late Cretaceous*
Where found: *Algeria, Egypt, Morocco*

Carcharodontosaurus will probably never be fully understood because its skeletal remains were destroyed by bombs in World War II. However, its shark-like teeth led many scientists to believe that this dinosaur may not have ripped the flesh of its prey, perhaps preferring smaller or softer animals than other carnivores of its size.

ACROCANTHOSAURUS
ack-roh-kan-thuh-sar-rus

Lizard HIPPED

Meaning: *High Backbone Lizard*
Group: *Therapoda*
Size: *30 feet long*
Time period: *Early Cretaceous*
Where found: *Oklahoma, Texas*

Another carnosaur was ***Acrocanthosaurus.*** Unlike Allosaurus and many other theropods, which had their heads positioned at the end of their S-shaped necks, Acrocanthosaurus's head jutted forward from a straight neck. Acrocanthosaurus also had a spine up to 17 inches long on its backbone.

Therapods

BARYONYX
bayr-ee-on-ix

Meaning: *Heavy Claw*
Group: *Therapoda*
Size: *30 feet long*
Time period: *Early Cretaceous*
Where found: *England*

Lizard HIPPED

Baryonyx had a long, low, "crocodile-like" snout with a spoon-shaped tip, long forelimbs, and very large foreclaws. Baryonyx was probably a fish-eater that waited on the shores of rivers to catch its meals.

CARNOTAURUS
kahr-nuh-tor-us

Meaning: *Flesh Bull*
Group: *Therapoda*
Size: *25 feet long*
Time period: *Mid to Late Cretaceous*
Where found: *Patagonia, Argentina*

Lizard HIPPED

A male ***Carnotaurus*** may have used its horns to intimidate other males, as do modern deer. The Carnotaurus with the largest "headgear" would have dominated the others.

Therapods

SPINOSAURUS
Spy-nuh-sar-rus

Meaning: *Spine Lizard*
Group: *Therapoda*
Size: *40 feet long*
Time Period: *Late Cretaceous*
Where found: *Egypt*

Turning its sail toward the sun, ***Spinosaurus*** could take in heat to warm up. Turning it away from the sun, the animal could throw off heat to cool down. The sail may also have been used by males to attract females.

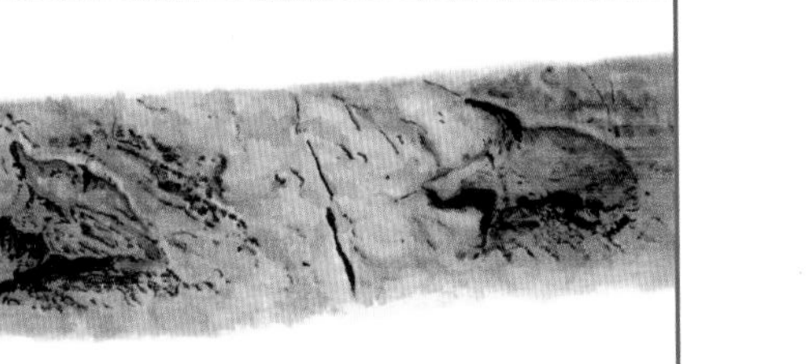

THERAPOD FOOTPRINTS

TROODON
troh-uh-don

Lizard HIPPED

Meaning: *Gnaw Tooth*
Group: *Therapoda*
Size: *6 feet long*
Time period: *Late Cretaceous*
Where found: *Montana, Wyoming, Alberta*

Troodon's large saucer-like eyes faced forward. They were not set on the sides of the head as were the eyes of most dinosaurs. This gave Troodon good vision and let the animal see in three dimensions. Because of its large brain, Troodon is regarded by some paleontologists as the smartest of all known dinosaurs.

Therapods

GALLIMIMUS
gal-i-my-mus

Lizard HIPPED

Meaning: *Chicken Mimic*
Group: *Therapoda*
Size: *17 feet long*
Time period: *Late Cretaceous*
Where found: *Gobi Desert, Mongolia*

From their long legs and stiff tails, it is obvious that the ***Gallimimus*** were fast runners—the fastest, in fact, of all running dinosaurs. Their speed came in handy not only for capturing small prey, but also for avoiding becoming the prey of larger meat-eating dinosaurs.

STRUTHIOMIMUS
stroo-thee-uh-my-mus

Lizard HIPPED

Meaning: *Ostrich Mimic*
Group: *Therapoda*
Size: *8 feet high*
Time period: *Late Cretaceous*
Where found: *Alberta*

Struthiomimus had long snouts, beak-like jaws covered with horny material, and big eyes. Toothless, and with long necks, these dinosaurs are the best known of the "ostrich dinosaurs." Their forelimbs and hands were weak and probably of little use in acquiring food—so most likely, these dinosaurs ate not only meat, but also insects, eggs, and plants.

Therapods

MONONYCHUS
mon-o-nye-kus

Meaning: *Single claw*
Group: *Therapoda*
Size: *3 feet long*
Time Period: *Late Cretaceous*
Where Found: *Mongolia*

Lizard HIPPED

There has been some scientific debate about ***Mononychus.*** The dinosaur has a fusion of bones in the arms that are quite similar to birds. However, since its arms of are very short and stoutly constructed, with only one, large, pointy digit, scientists have argued that Mononychus was secondarily flightless—meaning it may have descended from an ancestor with full flight capability.

AVIMIMUS
ah-vee-mim-us

Meaning: *Bird Mimic*
Group: *Therapoda*
Size: *About 5 feet long*
Time period: *Late Cretaceous*
Where found: *Mongolia*

Avimimus, one of the long-legged, birdlike dinosaurs, is thought to be among the fastest of all dinosaurs. With its slender body, long neck and birdlike feet, the Avimimus is believed to have caught insects and small reptiles for its food.

Therapods

DEINONYCHUS

di-no-ny-kus

Meaning: *Terrible Claw*
Group: *Therapoda*
Size: *About 10 feet long and 3 feet high*
Time period: *Early Cretaceous*
Where found: *Montana, Wyoming*

Deinonychus had a long tail, which it held out stiffly behind its body with a bundle of bony rods. This tail kept its body balanced when it walked or ran. Deinonychus was also a capable hunter—its eyesight was sharp—all the better to seek out its prey. The "killer claws" on its feet were designed as deadly offensive weapons.

A pack of *Deinonychus* attacking a *Tonantosaurus.*

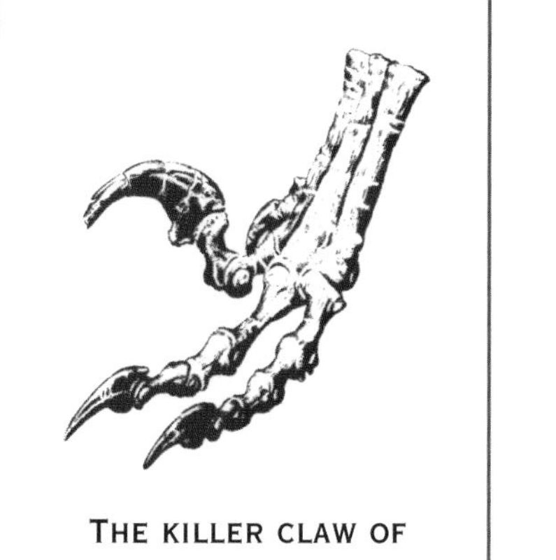

THE KILLER CLAW OF DEINONYCHUS

Therapods

OVIRAPTOR
oh-vi-rap-tor

Meaning: *Egg Robber*
Group: *Therapoda*
Size: *6 feet long*
Time period: *Late Cretaceous*
Where found: *Gobi Desert in Mongolia*

Most likely, ***Oviraptors*** were not hunters. Once believed to steal eggs for food, Oviraptors may have actually eaten insects and plants as well as scavenged flesh from dead animals. Their skulls were small and light, but their jaws were extremely strong and worked like powerful hedge clippers. These jaws were ideal for cutting through the tough leaves and other vegetation that grew when these dinosaurs lived.

ORNITHOMIMUS
or-ni-thuh-my-mus

Lizard HIPPED

Meaning: *Bird Mimic*
Group: *Therapoda*
Size: *12 feet long and 7 feet high*
Time period: *Late Cretaceous*
Where found: *Colorado, Utah, Wyoming, Montana, Alberta*

With long legs and lightly built skeletons, ***Ornithomimus*** was capable of reaching speeds of at least 25 miles per hour, making it one of the fastest in a family of bird-like dinosaurs. Weakly developed jaw muscles have led scientists to believe that this dinosaur may have dieted on eggs and soft-bodied animals.

Therapods

VELOCIRAPTOR
ve-los-i-rap-tor

Meaning: *Swift Robber*
Group: *Therapoda*
Size: *6 feet long*
Time period: *Late Cretaceous*
Where found: *Mongolia*

Lizard HIPPED

Velociraptor was swift, smart, and equipped with sharp teeth, large eyes, and long clawed fingers and toes. Its most distinguishing and frightening feature was a sickle-like claw on the second toe of its hind foot, which was used as a slashing weapon for attack.

DROMAEOSAURUS
droh-mee-uh-sar-us

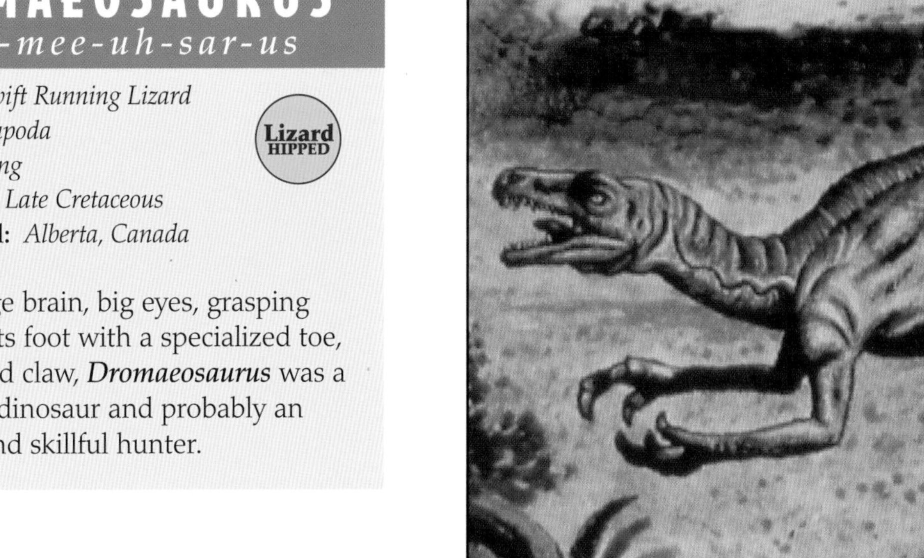

Meaning: *Swift Running Lizard*
Group: *Therapoda*
Size: *6 feet long*
Time period: *Late Cretaceous*
Where found: *Alberta, Canada*

Lizard HIPPED

With its large brain, big eyes, grasping hands, and its foot with a specialized toe, and oversized claw, ***Dromaeosaurus*** was a fleet-footed dinosaur and probably an intelligent and skillful hunter.

Therapods

GORGOSAURUS
gor-go-sar-us

Lizard HIPPED

Meaning: *Fierce Reptile*
Group: *Therapoda*
Size: *25 to 30 feet long*
Time period: *Late Cretaceous*
Where found: *Western North America*

Gorgosaurus had a narrow, huge head with one eye on each side and sharp, serrated teeth for sawing meat. It had two-fingered hands and its arms were longer than Tyrannosaurus's stubby forelimbs. This animal was a fast runner with a sleek build, and long hind limbs.

DASPLETOSAURUS
das-plee-tuh-sar-us

Lizard HIPPED

Meaning: *Frightful Lizard*
Group: *Therapoda*
Size: *25 to 30 feet long*
Time period: *Late Cretaceous*
Where found: *Albeta, Canada*

This enormous carnivorous dinosaur had a large head and small horns above and behind the eyes. ***Daspletosaurus***' forelimbs were longer than Gorgosaurus's , and the upper part of its foot was slightly shorter. The heavy, powerful Daspletosaurus lived in marshlands adjacent to streams, an environment also inhabited by horned dinosaurs, which they hunted.

Therapods

GIGANTOSAURUS
Gye-gan-tuh-sar-us

Meaning: *Giant Lizard*
Group: *Therapoda*
Size: *Very Large*
Time period: *Late Jurassic*
Where found: *England*

Lizard HIPPED

Little is known about *Gigantosaurus*, but because of the size of the few bones found, scientists imagine this dinosaur as huge, hence its name. Its fibula, the larger of the two bones in the lower hind limb, measure over two feet long.

TYRANNOSAURUS
tye-ran-uh-sar-us

Meaning: *Ruler Lizard*
Group: *Therapoda*
Size: *40 feet long*
Time period: *Late Cretaceous*
Where found: *North America and Asia*

Lizard HIPPED

Tyrannosaurus is the most famous of all theropods, and perhaps the most popular dinosaur of all. It may not have been the biggest carnivorous dinosaur, but it was certainly among the largest and most powerful land carnivores that ever lived. Tyrannosaurus appears to have had keen senses that aided him in his hunting. He is believed to have been an active predator, capable of achieving speeds as high as 25 miles per hour, in short bursts. The powerful hind limbs were designed not just for speed, but also for bearing great weight and perhaps for holding down large prey.

Skull of Tyrannosaurus Rex

Ornithopods

HYPSILOPHONDON
hip-suh-loh-fuhn-don

Meaning: *Iguana Tooth*
Group: *Ornithopoda*
Size: *7.5 feet long*
Time period: *Early Cretaceous*
Where found: *England, Spain, Portugal*

Bird HIPPED

This small, fast-moving dinosaur was lightly built and stood low to the ground. With its body held horizontally, it would have measured only 2 feet at the hips. ***Hypsilophondon*** had sharp, arched hind claws and powerful hind limb muscles. Its tail was long, and kept rigid by bony tendons attached to its tail vertebrae. These features are suited to fast running.

TENONTOSAURUS
te-non-tuh-sar-us

Meaning: *Sinew Lizard*
Group: *Ornithopoda*
Size: *23 feet long*
Time period: *Early Cretaceus*
Where found: *Montana, Wyoming, Utah, Texas, Ohlahoma*

Bird HIPPED

Tenontosaurus was a large plant-eater that not only moved on two legs, but also on all four. Tenontosaurus probably utilized a bipedal stance for rapid walking, and came down onto all four legs to stand, walk at a slower pace, or feed on low vegetation.

Ornithopods

MUTTABURRASAURUS
mut-uh-bur-uh-sar-us

Bird HIPPED

Meaning: *Muttaburra (township in Australia) Lizard*
Group: *Ornithopoda*
Size: *24 feet long*
Time period: *Lower Cretaceous*
Where found: *Australia*

Muttaburrasaurus was a large plant-eater with a flat snout. Its head was distinguished by a bumplike rise between its snout and eyes. This dinosaur's teeth seem to have worked like a pair of shears and may have been partially carnivorous.

IGUANODON

i-gwan-uh-don

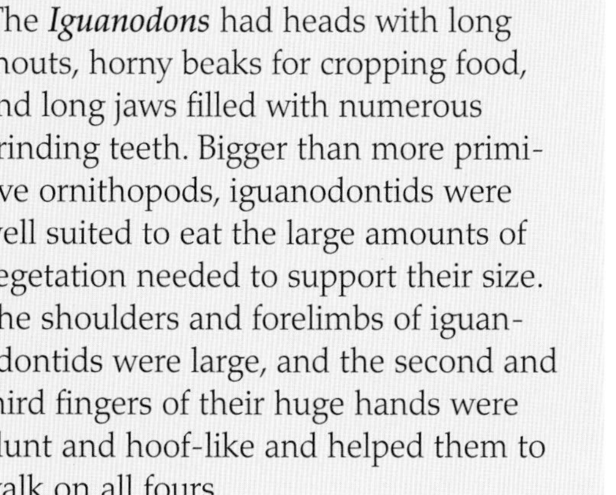

Meaning: *Lizard Tooth*
Group: *Ornithopoda*
Size: *33 feet long*
Time period: *Early Cretaceous*
Where found: *Europe and North America*

The ***Iguanodons*** had heads with long snouts, horny beaks for cropping food, and long jaws filled with numerous grinding teeth. Bigger than more primitive ornithopods, iguanodontids were well suited to eat the large amounts of vegetation needed to support their size. The shoulders and forelimbs of iguanodontids were large, and the second and third fingers of their huge hands were blunt and hoof-like and helped them to walk on all fours.

Ornithopods

Hadrosaurus being attacked by *Gorgosaurus*.

Ornithopods

HADROSAURUS
had-ruh-sar-us

Bird HIPPED

Meaning: *Sturdy Lizard*
Group: *Ornithopoda*
Size: *25 feet long*
Time period: *Late Cretaceous*
Where found: *Haddonfield, New Jersey*

Hadrosaurus is an historic, though average-sized hadrosaur, or duckbill. It belongs to the subfamily of duckbills, those with flat heads. It was the first dinosaur in the world known from a nearly complete skeleton. Hadrosaurus was believed to be a mostly amphibious animal that spent some time browsing on land, maintaining a kangaroo-like posture, resting on its hind legs and tail.

CORYTHOSAURUS
kor-ith-uh-sar-us

Bird HIPPED

Meaning: *Corinthian Helmet Lizard*
Group: *Ornithopoda*
Size: *30 feet long*
Time Period: *Late Cretaceous*
Where found: *Alberta, Canada*

The duckbill ***Corythosaurus*** is easily distinguished by the feature for which it was named—the helmet-like crest atop its head, resembling the helmet of a Corinthian soldier. The head of Corythosaurus is high, narrow, and "compressed" from side to side. It is believed that the crest in Corythosaurus served functions such as smelling and sound production and could have served as a visual display for identification purposes.

Ornithopods

Gorgosaurus persuing a *Hypocrosaurus*.

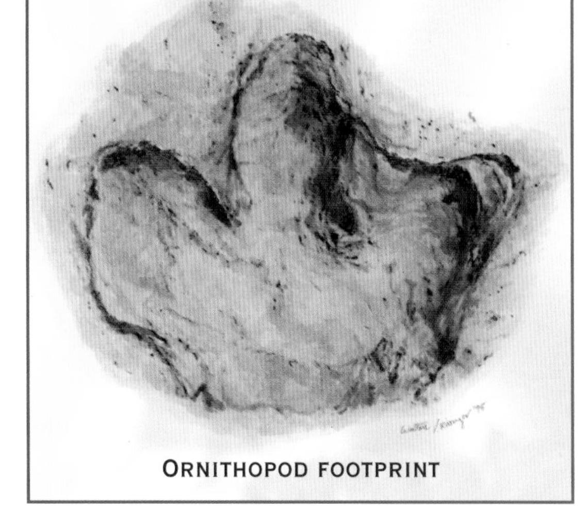

ORNITHOPOD FOOTPRINT

HYPACROSAURUS

hye-pack-ruh-sar-us

Bird HIPPED

Meaning: *Very High Lizard*
Group: *Ornithopoda*
Size: *30 feet*
Time Period: *Late Cretaceous*
Where found: *Alberta, Canada; Montana, USA*

Hypacrosaurus was a large duckbilled dinosaur of the hollow-crested, or hadrosaurid, family. It featured a helmet style, tall, narrow crest. Its skull was short and high, with a narrow muzzle. It had nearly forty rows of teeth in dental batteries, and a short, toothless beak. It also had a ridged back formed of elongated spines on its vertebrae.

Ornithopods

MAIASAURA
mye-uh-saw-ruh

Bird HIPPED

Meaning: *Good Mother Lizard*
Group: *Ornithopoda*
Size: *30 feet long*
Time period: *Late Cretaceous*
Where found: *Montana*

Maisaura were a subfamily of duckbilled dinosaurs and had a long, wide face with a short, wide bill. Maisaura families traveled together and were the first known dinosaur families. This dinosaur cared for its young in the nest until they were old and large enough to take care of themselves.

PARASAUROLOPHUS
par-uh-saw-ruh-loh-fus

Bird HIPPED

Meaning: *Lizard Crest*
Group: *Ornithopoda*
Size: *30 feet long*
Time Period: *Late Cretaceous*
Where found: *Alberta, Canada; Utah, Montana, USA*

Parasaurolophus may have weighed more than two tons. It was built to walk on all fours as well as on two legs. It is distinguished by its skull crest, an elongated, curved structure longer than the entire skull. Housed within the crest were two hollow tubes that ran to the far end and looped back again.

THE SKULL OF PARASAUROLOPHUS

Ceratopsians

BAGACERATOPS
bag-a-ser-ur-tops

Meaning: *Small Horned Face*
Group: *Ceratopsia*
Size: *3 feet long*
Time period: *Late Cretaceous*
Where found: *Mongolia*

Bird HIPPED

Bagaceratops was a small and primitive horned dinosaur with a short frill over its neck, which may have been laced with openings. Its snout was short, and had a small nose horn. Skulls of this dinosaur were discovered in the Gobi Desert of Mongolia.

BRACHYCERATOPS
brack-i-ser-uh-tops

Meaning: *Short Horned Face*
Group: *Ceratopsia*
Size: *6 feet long*
Time period: *Late Cretaceous*
Where found: *Montana*

Bird HIPPED

Brachyceratops was a small horned dinosaur with diminutive brow horns and a slight upward curve on its nose horn. Its frill had a scalloped border and a relatively sharp crest in the middle—an area perhaps pierced with small openings. Five small Brachyceratops were found near an adult dinosaur nearly twice their size, suggesting this may have been a family of young horned dinosaurs cared for by a parent.

Ceratopsians

PACHYRINOSAURUS
pack-i-rye-nuh-sar-us

Meaning: *Thick nose lizard*
Group: *Ceratopsia*
Size: *23 feet long*
Time period: *Late Cretaceous*
Where found: *Alberta, Canada; Alaska*

Bird HIPPED

Pachyrhinosaurus was the largest of all the short-frilled, horned dinosaurs, the centrosaurines. Pachyrhinosaurus had a large, rectangular skull that narrowed rapidly to a beak. The presence of a low bump in the nasal area was an unusual feature in Pachyrhinosaurus. This bump may have been utilized in matches with rival individuals.

STYRACOSAURUS
stye-rack-uh-sar-us

Meaning: *Spear Shaft Lizard*
Group: *Ceratopsia*
Size: *18 feet long*
Time period: *Late Cretaceous*
Where found: *Alberta, Canada; Montana, USA.*

Bird HIPPED

Styracosaurus was a relatively small horned dinosaur, a four-legged browser, weighing two or three tons. Its massive, elongated skull was pointed at the front and greatly extended behind to form a distinctive neck frill. The fear caused by this spiked head could have eliminated the need for direct physical combat during contests.

Ceratopsians

TOROSAURUS
tor-uh-sar-us

Meaning: *Protuberance lizard*
Group: *Ceratopsia*
Size: *21 feet long*
Time period: *Late Cretaceous*
Where found: *Wyoming, Utah, South Dakota, Montana, New Mexico, Texas; Saskatchewan*

Torosaurus was a very large horned dinosaur, distinguished by having, at 9 feet, the largest skull of any animal that ever lived on land. It was one of the last and most advanced of all ceratopsids, the large horned dinosaurs.

PROTOCERATOPS
proh-tuh-ser-uh-tops

Meaning: *First Horned Face*
Group: *Ceratopsia*
Size: *8 feet long*
Time Period: *Late Cretaceous*
Where found: *Mongolia*

Protoceratops was a small horned dinosaur with a triangular head, long tail, and feet adapted to walking on all fours. Protoceratops is one of the most common and best known of all dinosaurs and is now known to be the largest and most advanced of a series of early horned dinosaurs.

Ceratopsians

AVACERATOPS
ay-vuh-ser-uh-tops

Bird HIPPED

Meaning: *Horned Face*
Group: *Ceratopsia*
Size: *7 feet long*
Time Period: *Late Cretaceous*
Where found: *Montana, USA*

Avaceratops was one of the smallest true horned dinosaurs. It had a solid neck frill. It represents the most complete dinosaur specimen ever collected from Montana's Judith River Formation, a major source of dinosaur remains.

CHASMOSAURUS
kaz-moh-sar-us

Bird HIPPED

Meaning: *Opening Lizard*
Group: *Ceratopsia*
Size: *17 feet long*
Time Period: *Late Cretaceous*
Where found: *Alberta, Canada; Texas, USA*

Chasmosaurus was a modest-sized, horned dinosaur. It had a long skull and its brow horns ranged from small and short to large, solid, backward-curving structures. This dinosaur had a smaller adult body than other large, horned dinosaurs, and very slender limb bones.

Ceratopsians

MICROCERATOPS
yye-kroh-ser-uh-tops

Meaning: *Small Horned Face*
Group: *Ceratopsia*
Size: *30 inches long*
Time period: *Late Cretaceous*
Where found: *China*

This child-sized plant-eater is one of the tiniest known dinosaurs. ***Microceratops*** was a lightly built, small-sized protocertopsid, or horned dinosaur with a short frill and slender forelimbs. Its unusually long forelimbs may have been used when walking, perhaps at a slower pace, on all fours.

DICEROTOPS
dye-ser-uh-tops

Meaning: *Two Horned Face*
Group: *Ceratopsia*
Size: *30 feet long*
Time period: *Late Cretaceous*
Where found: *Wyoming, USA*

Dicerotops is classified as a horned dinosaur. It had two large horns over the eyes but none over its snout. Dicerotops is considered to be a rare horned dinosaur.

Ceratopsians

CENTROSAURUS SKELETON

CENTROSAURUS
sen-tru-sar-us

Bird HIPPED

Meaning: *Horned Lizard*
Group: *Ceratopsia*
Size: *17 feet long*
Time period: *Late Cretaceous*
Where found: *Alberta, Canada*

Centrosaurus had a pair of bony hooks pointing forward from the upper border of its frill and a long nose horn that sometimes curved forward. This heavily decorated dinosaur had two small horns above the eyes and one large horn over the snout. The animals travelled in herds as do cattle today.

TRICERATOPS
trye-ser-uh-tops

Bird HIPPED

Meaning: *Three Horned Face*
Group: *Ceratopsia*
Size: *30 feet long*
Time period: *Late Cretaceous*
Where found: *Colorado, Wyoming, Montana, South Dakota, USA; Alberta and Saskatchewan, Canada*

The three-horned plant-eater, ***Triceratops,*** is the largest, most common, and best known of the horned dinosaurs. It may have weighed 5 tons. Triceratops were heavy animals that walked on all fours—although smaller, more primitive ceratop-sians walked on their hind legs only. They lived only during the Late Cretaceous and were among the last dinosaurs to die out at the end of that period.

Armor

ANKYLOSAURUS
ang-kye-luh-sar-us

Meaning: *Curved, Crooked, or Bent Lizard*
Group: *Ankylosauria*
Size: *25 feet long*
Time period: *Late Cretaceous*
Where found: *Montana, Wyoming, USA; Alberta, Canada*

Bird HIPPED

Ankylosaurus is among the best known of all the armored, club-tailed dinosaurs from its family—the ankylosaurids. It was built low to the ground and its armor extended to the animal's bony eyelids, which worked like window shades to protect the eyes from attackers. Its tail club was a formidable weapon.

Armor

EUOPLOCEPHALUS
yoo-oh-pluh-sef-uh-lus

Bird HIPPED

Meaning: *Well-protected Head*
Group: *Ankylosauria*
Size: *17 feet long*
Time period: *Late Cretaceous*
Where found: *Alberta, Canada*

Euoplocephalus was armored from head to tail and its entire back and sides were covered with bony plates. These plates were smaller at the midsection and back of the animal and larger on its front and on the sides.

NODOSURUS
noh-duh-sar-us

Bird HIPPED

Meaning: *Knob Lizard*
Group: *Ankylosauria*
Size: *20 feet long*
Time period: *Late Cretaceous*
Where found: *Wyoming, Kansas, USA*

Nodosurus was a bulky creature with massive, powerful front limbs, which had five well-developed digits. Its tail seems to have been slender, flexible, and about half the length of the trunk. Nodosaurus's armor covered its sides and these plates were arranged in a series of rows. The external surface of the armor was marked by a pattern that appears interwoven.

Pachycephalosauria

HOMOCEPHALE
ho-mo-suh-fel-ee

Meaning: *Level-headed lizard*
Group: *Pachycephalosauria*
Size: *5 feet long*
Time period: *Late Cretaceous*
Where found: *Mongolia*

Bird HIPPED

Homalocephale was a thick-headed plant eater with a flat head, small brain, and large eyes. It was believed to have been a herding dinosaur that lived in groups, and flank-butting with its hard skull was probably its first line of self defense.

PACHYCEPHALOSAURUS
pack-ee-cef-uh-low-sar-us

Meaning: *Thick head lizard*
Group: *Pachycephalosauria*
Size: *15 feet long*
Time period: *Late Cretaceous*
Where found: *Montana, Myoming, South Dakota, USA*

Bird HIPPED

Pachycephalosaurus was the largest and most advanced of the bone-heads or pachycephalosaurs. This was a rare group of plant-eating, short-faced, bipedal dinosaurs. Its members were called bone-headed because of their thickened skull roofs. They had a narrow face, leaf-shaped teeth, and an extremely thickened skull roof, liberally studded with bumps. Its skull cap was decorated with various sized spikes.

Pachycephalosauria

PRENOCEPHALE
pree-no-sef-uh-lee

Bird HIPPED

Meaning: *Face Downwards*
Group: *Pachycephalosauria*
Size: *7 feet long*
Time period: *Late Cretaceous*
Where found: *Mongolia*

Prenocephale had large, forward-directed eyes and was believed to have superb vision. Although it was a plant eater, this bone-headed dinosaur was well suited to use its head for butting rivals.

STEGOCERAS
steg-os-uh-rus

Bird HIPPED

Meaning: *Roof Horn*
Group: *Pachycephalosauria*
Size: *7 feet long*
Time period: *Late Cretaceous*
Where found: *Alberta, Canada; Montana, USA*

Stegoceras was a small two-legged, thick-headed, plant-eater. It was small to medium-sized for a pachycephalosaurid. The dense dome on top of its head may have been used in head-butting contest for courting and/or social dominance. Much of this combat may have been flank-butting, not head-to-head ramming. Stegoceras's curved skull did not allow for easy head-to-head confrontation.

Why aren't there any dinosaurs around today?

Dinosaurs were indeed among the most successful animals the world has ever seen. But approximately 65 million years ago, something significant happened on Earth, affecting the global climate, landscape, oceans, animals, and plants. It was the end of the Mesozoic Era, and with it, the end of the age of Dinosaurs.

Scientists are still unsure as to exactly what happened, but we do know that at the end of the Cretaceous period, no new dinosaurian groups ever appeared. Extinction may have been a very slow process, taking millions of years, with the last of the animals ultimately unable to adapt to the many changes in their world. The continents were moving (causing new wind and ocean currents, and, consequently, a cooling climate). New woodland plants were appearing that were not suited to the dinosaur diet, and even diseases were spreading as dinosaurs wandered from one land to another.

The fire ball of an asteroid marked the end of the dinosaur age.

The final extinction may have been relatively sudden, caused by some cataclysmic force, such as the collision of some giant celestial object with the Earth. According to the most popular theory, an enormous asteroid or comet some 6 to 9 miles across, hit our planet at the end of the Cretaceous period. Supposedly, this impact created a dust cloud that darkened the sky.

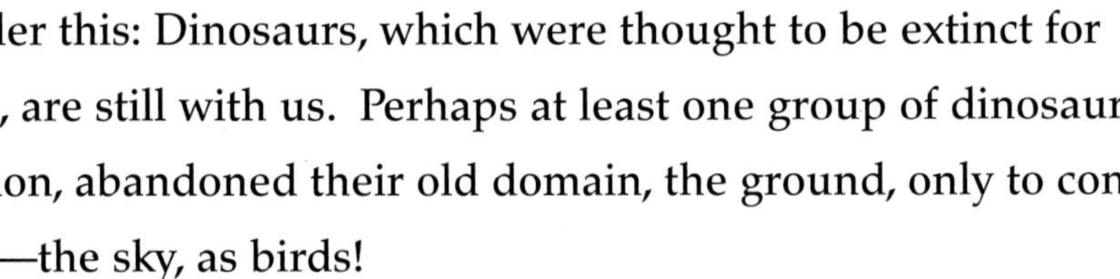

This loss of sunlight killed off many of the plant species that herbivorous dinosaurs ate. This disrupted the food chain and left the plant-eaters without food. As they began to die, so did the meat-eaters that preyed on the plant-eaters. According to this theory, all dinosaurs perished within a short period of time—possibly years or even months.

Both extinction theories have their flaws. For example, not all the animals that lived at the end of the Cretaceous became extinct. Why did some animals die and not others? Also, dinosaur bones found in polar regions, where the night can last for half a year, show that these animals were perfectly adapted to surviving in long periods of darkness.

Perhaps the final extinction was the result of a number of factors working together. But is the extinction of the dinosaurs really that important? Considering their long reign, their demise is not nearly as fascinating as their success. And keep in mind that most dinosaur paleontologists believe that birds descended from small therapods, much like Compsognathus. In fact, using modern methods of classification, all birds are considered to be members of the theropod group Maniraptora.

So consider this: Dinosaurs, which were thought to be extinct for 65 million years, are still with us. Perhaps at least one group of dinosaurs escaped extinction, abandoned their old domain, the ground, only to conquer a new one—the sky, as birds!